East & West Midlands

Edited by Annabel Cook

YoungWriters
First published in Great Britain in 2007 by:
Young Writers
Remus House
Coltsfoot Drive
Peterborough
PE2 9JX
Telephone: 01733 890066
Website: www.youngwriters.co.uk

SB ISBN 978-1 84602 882 3

Foreword

Young Writers was established in 1991 and has been passionately devoted to the promotion of reading and writing in children and young adults ever since. The quest continues today. Young Writers remains as committed to the nurturing of poetic and literary talent as ever.

This year's Young Writers competition has proven as vibrant and dynamic as ever and we are delighted to present a showcase of the best poetry from across the UK and in some cases overseas. Each poem has been selected from a wealth of *A Pocketful Of Rhyme* entries before ultimately being published in this, our fourteenth primary school poetry series.

Once again, we have been supremely impressed by the overall quality of the entries we have received. The imagination, energy and creativity which has gone into each young writer's entry made choosing the poems a challenging and often difficult but ultimately hugely rewarding task - the general high standard of the work submitted ensured this opportunity to bring their poetry to a larger appreciative audience.

We sincerely hope you are pleased with this final collection and that you will enjoy *A Pocketful Of Rhyme East & West Midlands* for many years to come.

Contents

Alfred Street Junior School, Rushden

Travis Davy (10)	1
Julian Tierney (11)	2
Lloyd Crook (11)	3
Rebecca Boult (10)	4
John Nicholson (10)	5
Koral De Grussa (10)	6
Rhyce Papp (10)	7
Ellie Beckett (10)	8
Jack Ebsworth (11)	9
Lucy Cottee (10)	10
Holly Hilson (10)	11
Shane Bale (10)	12

Blue Coat CE(A) Junior School, Walsall

Khuram Iqbal (10)	13
Maariya Hussain (8)	14
Danish Dharmaraj (9)	15
Lakesha Harris (9)	16
Madiha Parvin (9)	17
Bethany Johnson (10)	18
Gianna Noble-Cunningham (10)	19
Avneil Singh Purba (9)	20

Brington Primary School, Little Brington

Charlotte Townley (7)	21
Charlie Godwin (7)	22
James Smith (9)	23
Harry Buller (8)	24
Rebeca Toro (9)	25
Zachary Coupland (8)	26
Jacob Masters (9)	27
Delilah Walton (9)	28
John Leyden (8)	29
Ciara Moore (8)	30
Alice Kelly (8)	31
Joshua Fitzhugh (10)	32
Amy Smith (8)	33

Harry Fisk (8) 34
Angharad Slinn (11) 35
James Grayson (8) 36
Annabel Smith (7) 37
Oliver Robson (7) 38
Amy Keon (7) 39
Katherine Waterhouse (7) 40
James Healey (7) 41
Emily Bass (11) 42
Joshua Morris (10) 43
Jessica Pearcey (10) 44
George Gooney (10) 45
Sebastian Graham (8) 46

Hobmoor Primary School, Yardley
Reece Williams (10) 47
Abbi Lee (10) 48
Emma Hart (10) 49
Kyle Keenan (10) 50
Kinza Khan (9) 51
Lucy Hulbert (10) 52
Ryan Walton (8) 53
Maddysson Sandra-Ann Claffey (9) 54
Taylor Cairns 10) 55
Joshua Anzani (7) 56
Gabrielle Ahmed (10) 57
Katrina Barrett-Welsh (9) 58
Hope Armstrong (9) 59
Jay McNally (10) 60
Katie Bryan (7) 61
Christine McEvoy (11) 62
Liam Murray (10) 63
Rebekkah Payne (8) 64
Conner Latta (8) 65
Louise Scarr (8) 66
Georgia Lawrence (9) 67
Jordan Taylor (7) 68
Aimee Clarke (10) 69
Jayson Singh (7) 70
Hisham Rahman Ali (8) 71
Jonathan Finnegan (9) 72

King Edwin Primary School, Edwinstowe
Jason Brennan (7) 73
Ryan Page (8) 74

Oakfield Primary School, Rugby
Lee Curtis (10) 75
Matthew North & Tynan Jones (10) 76
Libby Hartly (10) 77
Travis Osborne (10) 78
Melissa Chamberlain (11) 79
Shannon Jaques & Shannon Ashby (10) 80
Amy Lee & Sabrina Cummings (10) 81
Ricky Pullen & Andrew Tone (10) 82
Daniel Batchelor (10) 83
Sadia Rahman (10) 84

Quinton House School, Upton
Luke Bonsey (7) 85
Molly Gray (11) 86
Stephanie Faghiri (10) 87
Elise Gallacher (8) 88
Daniel Hamid (8) 89
Jason Wilson (8) 90
Jessica Alvarez (10) 91
Alice Frost (10) 92
Tabitha Hunt (9) 93
Charlie Wright (10) 94
Camille Ling (10) 96
Jocelyn Rogers (9) 97
Robert Peat (9) 98
Antoinette Cassidy (7) 99
Piers Rogers (7) 100
Hugo Rogers (7) 101
Vinal Patel (7) 102
Oliver Strickland (7) 103
Benjamin Willingham (7) 104
Ellie Horton (9) 105
Sally Newton (10) 106
Oliver Bates (10) 107
Jia Chadha (9) 108

St Joseph's RC Junior School, Nuneaton

Sophie Blurton (9) 109

St Peter's CE Primary School, Market Bosworth

Emily Roberts (10) 110
Hannah Williamson (11) 111
Scott Cumbley (10) 112
Hannah Ingham (9) 113
Renee Allen (10) 114
Samuel Ingham (9) 115
Niamh Gascoyne (9) 116
Mary Pegg (8) 117
Ben Swan (10) 118
Sophie Lacey (9) 119
Emma Francis-Scott (10) 120
Abigail Cresswell (9) 121
Lucy Sandford-James (10) 122
Jessica Hurst (7) 123
Romey Kinsella (7) 124
Anna Sandford-James (10) 125
Helena Parkes (10) 126
Owen Hills (10) 127
Harriet Ball (9) 128
Harry Saunders (9) 129
Luke Batham (9) 130
Curtis Taylor (9) 131
Peter Harle (10) 132
Darcie Finn (7) 133
Chloe McDougall (10) 134
Joseph Bibby (9) 135
Sam Marston (9) 136
Ali Clinton (10) 137

Shipston-On-Stour J&I School, Shipston-On-Stour

Kelly Pyne (10) 138
James Hudson (10) 139
Ellie Turner (10) 140
Olivia West (10) 141
Emily Jennings (11) 142

Stanley Road Primary School, Worcester
Erinn Melville (8) 143
Sadikur Rahman (8) 144
Alizah Parveen Ghalib (7) 145
Sam Savage (8) & Joseph Sartain (7) 146
Ryan Brookes (8) 147
Jacob Moseley (8) 148

The Ferncumbe CE Primary School, Hatton
Charlotte May (10) 149
Tazmin Pinfold (9) 150
Ben Johnson (10) 151
Naomi Cruden (11) 152
Connor Henman (10) 153
Amelia Morris (9) 154
Daniel Ingall-Tombs (10) 155

Winterfold House School, Chaddesley
Harriet Goucher (8) 156
Phoebe Lydon (10) 157
Lydia Brindley (11) 158
Sophie Grenfell (10) 160
Mary Shinner (10) 161
Sam Price (10) 162
Sam Young (9) 163
Adam Grenfell (9) 164
Jordan White (10) 165
Katie Jeffries (9) 166
Elliott Hunt (9) 167
Jess Morris (11) 168
George Goucher (9) 169
Joseph Taylor (10) 170
Benjamin Melamed (10) 171
Christian Weston (9) 172
Elliott Price (9) 173
Axel Taylor (9) 174
Matthew Bubb (9) 175
Alesha Kettle (10) 176
Harry Hawkeswood (10) 177

Jack Barwell (9) 178
Cameron Bales (9) 179
Joseph Stringer (9) 180
Luke Staniland (10) 181

The Poems

Little Chicken's Long Stroll

There was a little chicken
Who crept into my kitchen
To eat some apple pie.
I chased him to the garden,
He ran into cement that was starting to harden.
He smashed through my fence,
That's when my muscles started to tense.
I yelled, 'Have some common sense!'
Running up the road,
Chasing after a toad.
He went to bed,
Thought he was dead.
He's asleep,
Not another peep.

Travis Davy (10)
Alfred Street Junior School, Rushden

Dog's Dinner

I once had a fish,
That fell into a dish,
In the middle of the day,
He had to go away.
So I served him with some noodles,
And gave him to my poodles.
I just watched and sat,
And that, well - that was that!

Julian Tierney (11)
Alfred Street Junior School, Rushden

Rugby

I'm playing rugby
It's real fun,
I like playing rugby
Getting all those bumps.

People are coming off,
People are injured,
People are getting rough.

It's getting calm,
Because of the ref.
I like it this way,
I don't get hurt.

Lloyd Crook (11)
Alfred Street Junior School, Rushden

Seasons

Spring is filled with life,
When baby animals are born.

Summer is filled with laughter,
When children are having fun.

Autumn is filled with magical things,
When spiderwebs are seen.

Winter is filled with cold, wet snow,
When children make snowmen.

Rebecca Boult (10)
Alfred Street Junior School, Rushden

Cars

Wheels turning,
Radio blaring,
Engine roaring,
Lights flashing,
Fast cars zooming,
Police car chasing,
Never-ending,
Two cars racing!

John Nicholson (10)
Alfred Street Junior School, Rushden

Lonely

My mum and dad have split up,
They kept arguing and upset me.
I got taken away from everyone, everyone except my soul.
I feel as lonely as a lost sheep.
I feel like nobody wants me, nobody cares anymore.
I wish we were a happy family, a family like we were.
Then I wouldn't be lonely,
Then I wouldn't be lonely again if I was with my mum.

Koral De Grussa (10)
Alfred Street Junior School, Rushden

Ten Things Found In My Drawer

One half-eaten chocolate bar (Galaxy),
One pair of smelly pants,
One mouldy wig (left over from Hallowe'en),
An eye from my teddy bear,
A letter from my teacher in mint condition,
One Yu-Gi-Oh card, a limited edition,
A packet of Pokémon cards,
A toy car,
One toy skeleton,
One tag glowing in the dark dog.

Rhyce Papp (10)
Alfred Street Junior School, Rushden

The Blitz

The sirens wail,
The bombers come,
Children run screaming,
Shouting for Mum.

War is something
Nobody likes,
A flash and a bang
With every bomb strike.

People run screaming,
Calling for help,
Into the shelter,
To sit this one out.

The bombers have gone,
We've got the 'All Clear'
This is the siren
We all want to hear.

Ellie Beckett (10)
Alfred Street Junior School, Rushden

Stars

Stars are twinkling in the sky,
Where everyone can see them.
I wish those clouds could drift away,
So stars could come on show.

Jack Ebsworth (11)
Alfred Street Junior School, Rushden

My Dad's Diet

About this time of year my dad goes on a diet,
I must admit it starts off well,
Until . . . until he sees the chocolate cake
That lies in the fridge,
Then it turns,
Turns into the *'see food eat it diet'!*
He will see food and eat it
He's like a Hoover, a bin, he scoffs it all in.
After that it starts again.
We will all sit down and he will say,
'I need to go on a diet!'
Now can you see what I mean.

Lucy Cottee (10)
Alfred Street Junior School, Rushden

Diamond Theft

Shiny and sparkly it may become,
It is just as shiny as a sparkling sun,
Being snatched by the hands of a thief,
Being mistaken for glass in the shape of a diamond.

The glass has been found - it was fake!
Diamond has been found in the lake.
The thief has been found,
And the diamond is safe once again.

Holly Hilson (10)
Alfred Street Junior School, Rushden

Thunder And Lightning

Thunder and lightning are scary,
One after one they light up the sky.
Lightning is an electric fork,
Thunder is God's hands clapping,
Thunder and lightning are a good team.

Shane Bale (10)
Alfred Street Junior School, Rushden

When I Was Really Scared

I'm really scared.
I smell odd smells everywhere I go.
Scary creatures following,
The smell got worse.
It wasn't very nice.
I'm really scared,
Am I seeing things?
Two eyes staring at me.
Help! Get away you night monster.

I'm really scared.
I saw a monster,
'Noooo!'
I yelled, 'Get away!'
I screamed for helped.

Khuram Iqbal (10)
Blue Coat CE(A) Junior School, Walsall

Friends

Friends are cool,
Friends are nice,
Friends are great to see
When we have bad times.

We should be good to everyone
That's how we make friends.
If I had no friends, I would be nice to everyone
This would help me make a lot of friends.
If we are nasty to everyone
Would we make friends?
No!

We are really lucky because we've got friends.
Friends are people who play with you,
Talk to you.
Friends are fun.

Maariya Hussain (8)
Blue Coat CE(A) Junior School, Walsall

The Scariest Day

Acid smells fill the air.
Shadows playing football?
Drip, drip, drip!
Is it dripping from the leaves?
Bang!

A shadow was dancing in the grass.
Hooo!
'Hi, I will get you,' it said.
A spell from the witch.
Oh no, I can't look back.

Danish! Danish!
Hiss - a creepy thing in a shadow moving across the grass.
What is that near the moon? A witch on a broom?
I can't see the moon again.

Suddenly the night vanished into morning.
The witch also disappeared.
The sun blazed across the sky.
I felt a little dizzy and fell to the ground.

Danish Dharmaraj (9)
Blue Coat CE(A) Junior School, Walsall

My Scary Night

Thunder struck. *Bang! Bang!*
On my window sill, it made me jump.
There it goes again.
A shadow seemed to dance.

Then I could hear footsteps.
Who . . . What could it be?
It's getting closer, it was the largest thing I've ever seen.
It had black eyes.
And it had very messy hair.
They turned on the light
And it was my mum. *Phew . . .*

Lakesha Harris (9)
Blue Coat CE(A) Junior School, Walsall

A Frightening Night

The first night in The Forest Of Dean.
My feet - cold as ice.
My body shivering.
What's that!

Oh maybe it's just a fox,
Glowing eyes looking at me.
A blue torch shining at me.
Somebody's hand's on my jacket - *Ahh!*
Or is that a twig?
The wind is blowing my tent.

Rain's falling from the sky into the pond,
Drip, drip, drip.
Yuck! What's that smell?
Disgusting. It smells like baby food,
And it smells like red roses mixed with mustard.

Suddenly . . . everything goes quiet and the smell has gone.
Fuh! beads of sweat fall down my face.

Madiha Parvin (9)
Blue Coat CE(A) Junior School, Walsall

A Hot Day

A hot day, a sandy beach,
The sand is covering my feet.
It is empty, no one on it - just me.

No water or food for me to eat.
No shade to cover me from the hot sun;
And the waves are splashing me.
Crashing onto the beach.

I can see shadows coming to haunt me.
Everything is blurry and hard for me to see.
There is sand for miles
And no one to see.

I can hear a chomping noise coming for me -
Chomp, chomp!
I must not look at it.
I can hear people calling me.
'Watch out,' people say to me.

Bethany Johnson (10)
Blue Coat CE(A) Junior School, Walsall

On The Way To School

On the way to school I pass a pool.
On the way to school I play pool.
On the way to school I swim in a pool.
On the way to school I love food.

Gianna Noble-Cunningham (10)
Blue Coat CE(A) Junior School, Walsall

A Stormy Night

I saw lightning flashing really fast
And clouds banging like fireworks high up in the sky.
I heard the clouds smashing like people stamping on the floor.
I'm scared, I want to go home . . .

I saw the clouds going grey
I heard big banging.
Was it lightning?
Was it a broken tree.
I'm scared, I want to go home . . .

I could smell broken eggs,
I could taste muddy water.
I'm scared, I want to go home . . .

Avneil Singh Purba (9)
Blue Coat CE(A) Junior School, Walsall

My Journey To School

Short cars driving to the park
Fluffy birds flying in the sky
Pretty flowers in a row
Long road on the path.

Charlotte Townley (7)
Brington Primary School, Little Brington

My Journey To School

Brown trees blowing about
Fluffy birds flying in the sky
Noisy cows eating grass
Blue sky moving about
Rabbits eating green land
Pigs eating green grass
Butterflies flying in the sky
Busy bees flying
Noisy horse galloping about
Whispering bugs
Burning sun in the sky
Wasps flying everywhere.

Charlie Godwin (7)
Brington Primary School, Little Brington

The Lighthouse

A spiralling spinning tower
A giant candle of tessellation
The guardian for the ships

An owl's head spinning around
The light shining across the sea
A big, blazing beacon.

James Smith (9)
Brington Primary School, Little Brington

Waves

Waves lapping on the sand
Waves smashing onto the rocks
Leaping tiger waves
A bolt of water
Smashing into the rocks
Bits falling off the rocks
Waves making currents
Waves making tidal waves
Making bombs.

Harry Buller (8)
Brington Primary School, Little Brington

Waves

Waves that dive
Waves that hide

Waves that are always
Cold and high

Waves you can surf on
Waves you can swim

Waves that are sometimes
Warm and tall!

Waves that are loud
Waves that are quiet

There are waves you can escape from
And waves you cannot

But remember all waves splash!

Rebeca Toro (9)
Brington Primary School, Little Brington

Waves

Waves, waves are monstrous, fierce and crazy
Waves, waves are imposing
Waves, waves are wet and salty
Waves, waves are pouncing tigers.

Zachary Coupland (8)
Brington Primary School, Little Brington

Waves

Waves that are pouncing lions
Waves that are kicking kangaroos
Waves that are vicious vipers
Waves that are diving dolphins
Waves that are springing spiders
Waves are the beasts of the sea.

Jacob Masters (9)
Brington Primary School, Little Brington

Waves

Waves that dive
Waves that splash
Waves that never stop smashing
Waves tall or small
Waves big and strong
Waves that bubble and crash
The fierce current flows with them
Their salty spray blows in the sea breeze.

Delilah Walton (9)
Brington Primary School, Little Brington

Waves

Waves that spill, dive and splash
Waves crash, smash, brash and mash
Waves break, froth and bubble
Waves rule the sea.

John Leyden (8)
Brington Primary School, Little Brington

Waves

Waves that are deadly
Waves that are strong
Waves that splash
Waves that don't
Waves that are little
Waves that dive.

Waves that are fierce
Waves that are soft
Waves that are crazy
Waves that are not
Some waves are lazy
Some waves are hot.

But every wave's different
And so are you.

Ciara Moore (8)
Bringtonn Primary School, Little Brington

Waves

Waves crashing and smashing on the beach
Waves fierce, angry, raging, a woken beast
Waves tired, slowing down.

Alice Kelly (8)
Bringtqn Primary School, Little Brington

The Lighthouse

The shining ships sailing the sea
The lighthouse protecting the three sailors.
A giant candle.

Joshua Fitzhugh (10)
Brington Primary School, Little Brington

Waves

Waves are wet and salty
Waves are strong and bubbly
Waves are crashing and slashing like glasses
Smashing on the ground
Waves are blue like the sky
Waves are like swooping birds that fly by.

Amy Smith (8)
Brington Primary School, Little Brington

Waves

Stormy waves hitting the rocks
Strong splashing waves
Waves moving boats
Waves as big as mountains.

Harry Fisk (8)
Brington Primary School, Little Brington

Waves

The waves that spill the yellow-sand shores,
The waves that scream, yell and roar,
The waves that dive in the ocean's sea,
The waves that give pleasure to you and me,
The waves that are vicious, pounding and tall,
The waves that are imposing but still quite small,
The waves that move like a tribal dance,
The waves that are claw-like and also prance,
The waves of the sea.

Angharad Slinn (11)
Brington Primary School, Little Brington

Waves

Waves are vicious, waves are strong,
Waves are gigantic, waves are huge,
Waves can be dangerous
Waves can kill
Waves can be imposing
Waves are pounding on my legs
Waves are crashing down
Waves are scary
Waves are tall.

James Grayson (8)
Brington Primary School, Little Brington

My Journey To School

Sweet friends at school
Hungry birds in the sky
Gigantic trees swaying softly
Lovely flowers in the meadows
Smelly cows getting milked
Grassy fields near the roads
Crooked walls fall to the ground
Small leaves falling off the trees.

Annabel Smith (7)
Brington Primary School, Little Brington

My Journey

Quiet island in the sea
Soft sand on the ground
Salty sea, very salty indeed
Slashing waves splashing about.

Oliver Robson (7)
Bringon Primary School, Little Brington

My Journey To School

Fruity food floating away
Breathless birds in the sky
Frilly flowers in a wedding
Trickling trees trembling
Fascinating fuel
Engines always on
Horrible berries very red
Lovely air in the sky.

Amy Keon (7)
Bringtón Primary School, Little Brington

My Journey To School

Fluffy birds in the sky
Leafy trees swaying in the air
Green grass in the field
Fast cars zooming
Noisy buses going along
Hard houses in the street
Shiny sun gleaming
Smelly cows in the farm.

Katherine Waterhouse (7)
Brington Primary School, Little Brington

My Journey To School

Smelly cows in the field
Fluffy birds singing in the trees
Hard houses in the street
Shiny sun gleaming in the sky
Red and yellow leaves falling on the ground
Green grass swaying in the breeze
Fast cars zooming along the road
Noisy buses roaring along the road.

James Healey (7)
Brington Primary School, Little Brington

Waves

They crash on beaches
Like fierce monsters.
They carry seaweed
In their currents.
They jump and dive in the sea.
They roar and scream and shout at me.
They pound on people
Who are in their midst.
They impose on the oceans.
They are the waves of the sea.

Emily Bass (11)
Brington Primary School, Little Brington

Waves

Waves glitter in the gleaming sun
Waves salty and strong
Waves tall and fierce
Waves like diving dolphins
Waves explode like bombs
Waves.

Joshua Morris (10)
Brington Primary School, Little Brington

Waves

I look out at the deadly pounding of the sea
The battling waves against the crazy current
Fighting
Fighting to win over the sea's ships
They claw in the sea
Killers
Devious predators.

Jessica Pearcey (10)
Bringtón Primary School, Little Brington

Waves

Waves in the morning, calm and quiet
As they roll gently into shore.
Waves getting busy
Waves getting fierce.

George Gooney (10)
Brington Primary School, Little Brington

Waves

Waves smashing on the rocks
Waves pushing people away
Salty sea in your mouth
Waves crashing on boats
Waves splashing everywhere
Waves bringing seaweed.

Sebastian Graham (8)
Bringston Primary School, Little Brington

About Pets

A bird's wings fluttering in the cage
Dog's ears flapping in the breeze
Cats crouching in the grass
Fish swimming all the time
Dog chasing cat to the tree
Cat fleeing a threatening man
Snake squirming in its home
Bird biting food still
Lizard laying low
My pets are troublemakers and money takers.

Reece Williams (10)
Hobmoor Primary School, Yardley

Moonlight's Frights

In the dark at night,
You're in for a fright.
If you don't stay safe,
You'll have to pay the price.
Don't be a fool,
Play it cool.
The robbers are out,
But don't scream and shout.
Don't go in an alley,
Or you'll get your finale.
Don't go in the park,
Where nasty people lurk.
Don't cross the road
As slowly as a toad.
So stay in at night,
Or you'll have a fright.
As dawn comes true,
Safeness is you!

Abbi Lee (10)
Hobmoor Primary School, Yardley

Miss You

I know I'm gonna miss you,
That much I know is true,
And I know what was done
Was the bestest thing for you.

Your cute little face
And your little tiny paws.
You make me smile Penny
You were the best hamster of all.

Now that you've gone,
My smile's changed to tears
But I'll always have the memories
Of when you were still here.

Emma Hart (10)
Hobmoor Primary School, Yardley

My Beloved Friend

I had a dog not long ago,
She died very suddenly.
I cried so much I thought I would die
To know my best friend had gone.

Every day I'd go out,
To see where my best friend was laid
My heart would ache for her once more.

The loss I felt was hard to bear
My dear beloved friend, I hope one day
We will be friends once more
And never shall be apart again
My beloved friend.

Kyle Keenan (10)
Hobmoor Primary School, Yardley

Muddy Puddles

Muddy puddles,
Cracking trees,
Gutters flooding,
Falling leaves.
Water spreading
People rushing,
Babies crying,
Children splashing,
Cold weather,
Warm clothes,
Dark nights,
That's how it goes.

Kinza Khan (9)
Hobmoor Primary School, Yardley

Sunshine

The bright shining,
Beaming in the crystal sky.
All the children are playing in the pool,
But I think I need an ice cream
So I can stay cool.

Lucy Hulbert (10)
Hobmoor Primary School, Yardley

Excuses, Excuses

Miss I was late because my brother had been sick.
Miss my dog bit me.
Miss my alarm clock broke.
Miss my house was on fire!
Miss my pet slug died.
Miss, a butterfly died and I cried and cried.
Miss I did a science experiment before school and it blew up.

Ryan Walton (8)
Hobmoor Primary School, Yardley

Rainbows

I like rainbows,
They are nice to see.
There are so many colours,
Shining down on me.

Red, yellow, green and blue,
My favourite colours I see.
These are just a few,
Shining down on me.

They all start off as white,
But this you do not see.
Filtering through the atmosphere,
Shining down on me.

There are so many colours,
For all of us to see.
But I like all of them,
Shining down on me.

Maddysson Sandra-Ann Claffey (9)
Hobmoor Primary School, Yardley

Colours

The colour blue,
Is the colour of
The sea and sky.

The colour red,
Is the colour of
The sun and lava.

The colour yellow,
Is the colour of
The bananas and light.

The colour green,
Is the colour of
The grass and leaves.

The colour brown,
Is the colour of
Wood and hair.

The colour black,
Is the colour of
The sky at night.

Taylor Cairns 10)
Hobmoor Primary School, Yardley

A Poem About Me

When I grow up big and strong,
And go to school every day,
I want to make the world a better place.
I want to train and get the job
I've always dreamed of having.
I'll do my best and try real hard.
I know one day I'll be that man to change the world
And be a policeman, and make the world feel safe.
I know I can if I try real hard.
I can make the world a better place to live in.

Joshua Anzani (7)
Hobmoor Primary School, Yardley

If You Ever Won The Lottery

If you ever won the lottery
What would you buy . . .?
'A place in Spain,' says Mum.
'A brand new car!' cries Dad.
'All the cute boy bands,' shouted my sister Melissa.
'I would buy a four-wheeled motorbike!' said I.
'We would buy a new settee!' cheered my nan and grandad.
But what would you buy?

Gabrielle Ahmed (10)
Hobmoor Primary School, Yardley

The Park

The sun comes up to make dawn light
And all the birds take flight.
The new fresh grass flowing in the breeze
Now smells like Febreeze.

The swings rattle in the wind,
The leaves begin to drop,
The clock calls 12 o'clock, it's dinner time
And the children drink their glass of lime.

Adults lay out their picnics and talk while they're doing that,
While children play together creating no harm.
I can see them playing hide-and-seek and maybe playing
a game of tig.
But most of all they're playing together and they're having
so much fun.

Katrina Barrett-Welsh (9)
Hobmoor Primary School, Yardley

Tubbie

Many little ears drooping low,
Sheepish eyes losing their glow.
Too many dogs needing a home
We would need a mansion as big as Rome.

Brown and cute she sat obediently,
Watching people pass by patiently.
I stooped by her cage,
She crept forward for a closer peep,
And then I knew she would be mine to keep.

Hope Armstrong (9)
Hobmoor Primary School, Yardley

Rhymes With Light

We all know there is light,
We all know it is bright.

Sparkly, shiny sunlight
On the sea is a lovely sight.

A boy is flying his kite,
He is holding it very tight.

There was a plane at its full height,
It was soaring through the night.

At school Jim had a fright,
When the teacher said none of his answers were right!

Jay McNally (10)
Hobmoor Primary School, Yardley

I Love Maths

Maths, maths I like maths, it's great fun.
I like to do maths every day.
You and me will do maths.
We do times, adding and my favourite, take away.

We play games in class,
We love games very much.
My favourite game is playing snakes and ladders
I roll the dice and it lands on six. I move a space.

Maths, maths I love maths, it's such fun to do.
I do maths every day.
I add, subtract, divide and my favourite, take away.

Katie Bryan (7)
Hobmoor Primary School, Yardley

The Dog Who Belongs To Me - Frank

The dog who sits in the corner
With bright shiny eyes.
Go over and pat his furry head.
The puppy face that calls you without a word
Knows when it is time for food and can't help but beg.
Till that food he is allowed to have
Rushing off he goes.
Till all the food has gone right down
Then it's time for bed.
The dog who sits in the corner
With bright shiny eyes.

Christine McEvoy (11)
Hobmoor Primary School, Yardley

Untitled

Leaves falling from the trees,
Creatures crawling in the leaves.
Snow falling from the sky
Onto the branches of the tree.
Leaves blowing from the trees,
Wind gushes and crazy as can be.
Sun hot, hot, hot as can be
Burning the trees.
Bush fire breathes, breathes, breathes.
The trees scream inside themselves,
Scream, scream, scream.
Chirp, chirp, the birds scream
As their nests shrivel and burn.

Liam Murray (10)
Hobmoor Primary School, Yardley

Excuses, Excuses

Sorry Miss the bus came late.
Sorry Miss I got up late.
Sorry Miss my brother bumped his head.
Sorry Miss I got in the shower late.
Sorry Miss I could not find my school bag.
Sorry Miss I could not find my lunch box.
Sorry Miss my dog ate my homework.
Sorry Miss my cat ripped my homework up.

Rebekkah Payne (8)
Hobmoor Primary School, Yardley

Excuses, Excuses

The bus was late,
My car broke down,
My sister's acting like a clown.
Alarm went off at half-past eight,
That's when I realised that I was late.
I got to school,
My teacher's mad,
I told her that it was my dad.
She told me off,
Sent me away,
Maybe I'll be on time one day.

Conner Latta (8)
Hobmoor Primary School, Yardley

Excuses, Excuses

Sorry I'm late.
My shoe got stuck in the gate,
My brother got his head stuck in the drawer,
My sister ran into the door.
So that made me late,
And I will never be late again.

Louise Scarr (8)
Hobmoor Primary School, Yardley

Excuses, Excuses

Sorry I'm late Miss,
My brother woke up late,
My mom forgot the date,
My dad forgot his keys,
I cut my knees,
My brother was hopping round the street happy,
Miss, my mom kept having to change the baby's nappy.
My dad's car broke,
He found out my sister was playing a joke,
My brother would not walk,
And my grandad stopped to talk.

Georgia Lawrence (9)
Hobmoor Primary School, Yardley

Going Swimming

At the swimming pool we have big slides,
They have showers, mini fountains with waterfalls
And a jacuzzi with bubbles.

We need to wear our swimming trunks and costumes
And wear our goggles over our eyes so they don't get water in them.

There are children wearing armbands to help them swim
And lifeguards on standby if you fall in.

Jordan Taylor (7)
Hobmoor Primary School, Yardley

Who's There?

I was on my own,
No one there
Except a shadow on the stair.
I called out, 'Who's there?'
No one replied except for a howl,
Murmur,
Wag of a tail
And a cough.
Who's there?
Who's there?
I don't know I wasn't there!

Aimee Clarke (10)
Hobmoor Primary School, Yardley

I'm Football Mad

Football mad, football mad, I'm football mad!
I play with my sister, she's not as good as me.
I pretend she's better but she can't balance a football on her knee!
I'm a Liverpool fan, I think they're the best,
I know I'll be their next man because I'm better than all the rest!
Football mad, football mad, I'm football mad!

Jayson Singh (7)
Hobmoor Primary School, Yardley

The Big Fat Ball Goes To The Park

The big fat ball was lonely
He couldn't find a boy to play with.
So he bounced to the nearest park to look for a boy.
When he found a boy, the boy was not alone,
He had a dog with him, the dog had taken the boy out for a walk.
The dog kept rushing to bring the stick to the boy
And the boy kept fit and happy, throwing the stick again and again.
The big fat ball rolled over to the dog
And the dog sniffed the big fat ball and nudged it with his nose
to the boy.
The boy kicked the big fat ball into the pond.
The boy's laugh became a moan of sadness,
The dog howled and jumped into the pond after the big fat ball.
He nudged the big fat ball towards the boy.
The boy reached down and picked up the big fat ball.
The boy was happy, the dog was happy
And the big fat ball was happy too.
Everyone was happy.

Hisham Rahman Ali (8)
Hobmoor Primary School, Yardley

School Is Cool

School is cool,
And I have a tool,
And it's called a brain
And I have stars to gain.
At break I have some chocolate,
I love art
And I love to take part.
Then at 2.30 it's playtime
Then it's the end of the day,
Then it's time to play.

Jonathan Finnegan (9)
Hobmoor Primary School, Yardley

Summer In Spain

Summer, summer, summer
Creamy ice cream and lollipops too.

Summer, summer, summer,
Hot sunny place like Spain.

Summer, summer, summer,
Waves for dinghies and speedboats.
Vroom, vroom, vroom
And off they go.

Summer, summer, summer,
Breezy sand you can make sandcastles
With shells and water.

Summer, summer, summer,
Hot deserts and brown coconuts on the trees.

Summer, summer, summer,
Flags flapping in the wind
Go eat ice cream on the beach
You can go on your holidays in the desert.

Summer, summer, summer,
Chocolate, ice cream -
Lovely chocolate melts when you put it in the sun.

Summer, summer, summer,
Paddling our feet in the warm sea.

Jason Brennan (7)
King Edwin Primary School, Edwinstowe

Winter Is

Winter is for sledging,
Winter is for snowballs,
Winter is for diamonds on cobwebs,
Winter is for frost and ice,
Winter is for making icicles,
Winter is for making snowmen.

Ryan Page (8)
King Edwin Primary School, Edwinstowe

Sadness

Sadness is like a blue teardrop
To clear it up you need a mop.
The wind is blowing soft
While I am in the loft.
Sadness tastes boring like lettuce,
It smells like funeral flowers,
It looks like a rainy day,
It feels like death.

Lee Curtis (10)
Oakfield Primary School, Rugby

Fruit And Veg

Fruit and veg are the best of friends,
They like to keep us children healthy,
Potatoes, carrots and all the rest,
They will make us strong as men,
They will make us fit and healthy
For the rest of our lives.

Matthew North & Tynan Jones (10)
Oakfield Primary School, Rugby

My Cat Is A Good, Cat

My cat is a good cat, yes she is.
My cat is a good cat, yes she is.
For she curls up small
And plays with her ball
And she chases her tail around the hall.
My cat is a good cat, yes she is.

Libby Hartly (10)
Oakfield Primary School, Rugby

The Cheetah

The cheetah is fast like a Ferrari.
You can hardly see it when it leaps for its prey.
At night it hides in bushes, attacking any passing animal.
When it is tired it sleeps in a tree,
The cheetah is the fastest animal on land.

Travis Osborne (10)
Oakfield Primary School, Rugby

Cats And Dogs

We had a cat with black and white spots
Who loved to play with tiny tots.
What the cat got up to, who knows what.
He always had a mischievous plot.
He ran about every day,
He ran up the street a different way.
He ran very fast,
Like a huge blast.
You would never see
That it was he.

We had a dog that was really strong,
He never knew what he did wrong.
He had a nice big blue eye,
When tired he'd give a big sigh.
He ran very fast,
He was never last.
He made people wet,
Whoever he met.
He swam in the pool,
To keep very cool.

The cat and dog had a chase,
The dog chewed up my blue shoelace.
That dog tripped me up!
What a bad pup!
They both settled down
Back in town
They played with tots,
Lots and lots.
Near the fire,
That's what I admire.

Melissa Chamberlain (11)
Oakfield Primary School, Rugby

Mystical Creatures

Tiptoeing and dancing through the night,
Pixies prancing in the moonlight.
Fairies floating, twirling, falling.
Dragons hurling and throwing their fire,
Having a unicorn would be my desire.
Annoying, green, pointy and sneaky, tiny little things.
Pink like roses, green and yellow.
Dwarfs and elves are little fellows.
Floating and breathless and never die.
Pointy hats and coloured skin,
Don't touch, you don't know where they've been.

Shannon Jaques & Shannon Ashby (10)
Oakfield Primary School, Rugby

Best Friends

Best friends do everything together,
We're best friends, whatever the weather.

If people tell tales about each other
We don't listen because we're best friends forever.

They don't fight at all, they believe each other,
They're best friends and they trust one another.

Amy Lee & Sabrina Cummings (10)
Oakfield Primary School, Rugby

Goals All Round

Chelsea, Man U, Arsenal, Liverpool
They get goals all round.
Arséne Wenger needs a special tool,
Man U will give Arsenal a pound
To win the golden cup this year.
The manager must go up a gear.

Ricky Pullen & Andrew Tone (10)
Oakfield Primary School, Rugby

Haunted House

A ghost is scary,
It comes after you.
A scary haunted house
With acrobats, cobwebs and spiders
And hooting owls all night.

An unexpected stranger came for a visit.
One night all the ghosts came out
And frightened her away with their haunting sound.

Daniel Batchelor (10)
Oakfield Primary School, Rugby

The Silver

Creeping slowly over the moon,
Coming closer really soon.
Over and under she peeps and sees,
Glowing chestnuts upon the trees.
Suddenly come a bird with a catch,
And hides beneath the silver hatch
Getting caught in the log
With a howl of sound, the sleeping dog.
From a shadowy breeze the light wind peeps
The lightening breeze always sleeps.
A flying dove goes slowly by
With silver claws and silver eyes.
A motionless fish always gleams
By silver reeds in silver streams.

Sadia Rahman (10)
Oakfield Primary School, Rugby

Mummy

My mummy's super,
My mummy rocks,
My mummy always
Wears pink socks.

My mummy works,
Does all the jobs,
She helps Josh
When he sobs.

My mummy's careful,
My mummy's nice,
My mummy is
Afraid of mice.

My mummy's the best,
My mummy's the best,
The best mummy in the world!

Luke Bonsey (7)
Quinton House School, Upton

Break Time Talk

Ella's swapping stickers,
Phoebe's trying to die,
Alice is going crazy,
Bella's eating pie.

Louie's playing football,
Bethany is mad,
Tom's burping loudly,
Stephanie is bad.

Harry has gone cross-eyed,
Molly has found bugs,
Andrea's very sick
Polly likes big hugs.

Amber's having a fit,
April's having fun,
Emma's playing netball,
May has a big bun.

Charlie's talking loudly,
June is very fast,
Fay is running around,
Jo is always last.

Molly Gray (11)
Quinton House School, Upton

In The Morning Break

Alice Cole is skipping,
Jodie's got her hoop,
I'm playing recorder,
Joe's trying to shoot.

Ella's playing netball,
Luke's climbing around,
Jessie's playing tag,
John's making a mad sound.

Kim is swapping stickers,
Lu's charging at Miss,
Lol is playing football,
Ben's trying to kiss.

Lulu's reading a book,
Tom is eating a snack,
Alana's run away,
Now she's coming back.

Ray is smacking Kevin,
Laura's crouching down,
April is now the queen,
Molly's got her crown.

Josh is trying to skip,
Max is killing snails,
Jack is telling bad jokes,
Lee's snipping off tails.

Fi's collecting conkers,
Emma's got her purse,
Alice cut her finger,
Now she needs the nurse.

Amber's got a nose bleed,
So have both the twins,
Josh is fighting Charlie,
Lucy's searching bins.

What a load of rubbish,
In my morning break.

Stephanie Faghiri (10)
Quinton House School, Upton

Images Of A Snail

The snail
    gobbles
like a shark hunting its prey for a lovely dinner,
        slithers
like a traffic jam ruining everyone's day,
        slumbers
like a broken television that's waiting to be repaired.

The snail's shell
    follows
like a shadow from the sun that never goes away,
        falls
like a frog trying to climb a brick wall,
        travels
like an aeroplane flying to India.

Elise Gallacher (8)
Quinton House School, Upton

Images Of A Snail

A snail
Slithers
Like a snowboard on slidey slippery ice.
Coils
Like a slug covered in salt on a spiral staircase.
Feasts
Like a great gobbling bin munching on some rubbish.

Daniel Hamid (8)
Quinton House School, Upton

Images Of A Spider

The spider
Blends
Into the background of the dark night.
Vicious
Like a hippopotamus ripping apart a crocodile.
Clever
Like a highwayman with a broken leg.

The spider's web
Catches
Like a fly at a cricket match.
Silent
Like the wind in the skies.
Thick
Like a weightlifting bar.

Jason Wilson (8)
Quinton House School, Upton

Morning Break

Ruby is killing Paul,
Gem's climbing the wall,
Emma is super kind,
Max is being small.

Sam's being super sad,
Tabby wants her mum,
Alice is pulling hair,
Ray's being dumb.

Harry's playing football,
Megan lost her rag,
Ella's swapping stickers,
Emma's playing tag.

Melanie is shouting,
Bethany's bonkers,
Evie's acting crazy,
Ray's getting conkers.

Melanie's in a mood,
Sam is being bad,
Katie's having a fit,
Molly's going mad.

Ellie fills her belly,
Jess is feeling sad,
Alice's rather funny,
Dan is being bad.

Sue's throwing a paddy,
Janine's in a strop,
Niki's crying loudly,
John cares not a jot.

Clare makes a daisy chain,
James is fighting Chris,
The sun's shining brightly
And Jane wants a kiss.

Jessica Alvarez (10)
Quinton House School, Upton

Morning Break

Gemma's swapping bright cards,
Emma's being weird,
Tim is pulling a fit,
Gary shaved his beard.

Stephanie is burping,
Josh is in the field,
Hassan is swapping stamps,
Ella's lips are sealed.

Ray is in a tantrum,
April wants her horse,
Alice is a dullard,
Molly's doing chores.

Harry's being a girl,
Louie cuts his hair,
Andrea's growing up,
Amber's in a stare.

All the girls are skipping,
Jane is at art club,
Beth is completely mad,
Charlie wants the pub.

We must get back to class,
We run past the lake,
To say goodbye now folks,
To a morning break!

Alice Frost (10)
Quinton House School, Upton

Under My Pillow

Where is it?

Last place to look,
Under my pillow,
PJs that I've worn for the last three weeks,
An odd stripy sock that really wreaks.
A scrap piece of paper, my old bookmark,
A torch for reading after dark.
A book that I finished yonks ago,
A curled up plaster from my toe.
A chewed old pen to write my dreams,
My one-eyed teddy ripped at the seams.
A crisp packet left from the last sleepover,
My good luck charm, a four-leafed clover.
My secret stash of chocolate yummies,
Cut up magazine of my mummy's.

Got it!
My nightie for tonight.

Tabitha Hunt (9)
Quinton House School, Upton

Break Time Snapshots

Bobby's playing football,
Jim's just spooned a shot,
Ash scored a cracking goal,
Sam has licked his snot.

Gemma's swapping stickers,
So is Laura too,
Jade is doing cartwheels,
Ben went to the loo.

Ellen's playing skipping,
John is playing tag,
Will is telling a joke
And Lennie wants a fag.

Omar's shouting loudly,
Kim is going nuts,
Sol's sobbing quietly,
Because he has some cuts.

Sally's drinking cola,
Simon's eating cake,
Dom is reading a book,
Tom jumped in the lake.

Terry stated singing,
Toby bit his nail,
Jerry sucked his big toe,
Max's bun is stale.

Tony's playing cricket,
Nathan is in bat,
Oliver is bowling,
Levi wants a cat.

Aaron's playing baseball,
Gary wants a go,
Chaz ran to the kitchen,
To make pizza dough.

William is fighting,
He's fighting with Rob,
Julie's playing robots,
Frank wants Uncle Bob.

Paul is playing Star Wars,
Shelly wants to bake,
Now the bell is ringing,
It's the end of break!

Charlie Wright (10)
Quinton House School, Upton

I Hate Autumn!

A chestnut tree with many conkers,
There are so many leaves it's driving me bonkers.

The wind and the rain are getting stronger,
I need to get in, I can't stand it for much longer.

There is a squirrel with a furry tail,
I can't stop thinking about it, it's making me go pale.

So I'm going in now, I'm shutting the door,
Closing the curtains and playing a game on the floor.

Camille Ling (10)
Quinton House School, Upton

Seasons

Newborn lambs
Babies in prams.

The blossom has come
Below the pale sun.

As the hot sun gleams
People are eating ice creams.

Everyone's splashing about in the sea
Everyone, everyone, even me.

Yellow, brown, orange, red
The leaves are falling on my head.

I can see conkers fall
From the trees very tall.

A snowball flies through the air
There's a white blanket everywhere.

People snuggle by the fire
The weather outside is really dire.

A season is a funny thing
Especially the things they bring.

But why are there seasons?

Jocelyn Rogers (9)
Quinton House School, Upton

Autumn

Leaves yellow, brown and red
Conkers falling on your head
While little moles are in their beds
The children are excited for Hallowe'en, *boo!*
Autumn is back and there is lots to do.

Robert Peat (9)
Quinton House School, Upton

Soundtrack For A Horror Film

The squeaking of the bats
The creaking of the door
The howling of the wind
The screaming of the children

The slamming of the planks
The singing of the ghosts
The scraping of the swords
The creaking of the windows

The cheering of the TV
The munching of the popcorn
The buzzing of the flies
The hissing of the vampire.

Antoinette Cassidy (7)
Quinton House School, Upton

A Weekday Morning

The clucking of the chickens
The barking of the dog
The music of the radio
The bubbling of the bacon

The hissing of the kettle
The creaking of the door
The miaowing of the cat
The munching of the cornflakes

The noise of the television
The running of the tap
The ringing of the telephone
The chiming of the clock.

Piers Rogers (7)
Quinton House School, Upton

A Building Site

The banging of the hammer
The slamming of the brick
The crashing of the digger
The sloshing of the cement

The splashing of the tap
The talking of the men
The creaking of the ladder
The crunching of the snacks

The splashing of the paint
The drilling of the drill
The puffing of the workers
The tapping of the rain.

Hugo Rogers (7)
Quinton House School, Upton

A Busy Morning

The popping of the toaster
The crying of the baby
The cuckoo of the clock
The turning of the key

The bashing of the toy
The cracking of the bowl falling
The splatter of the milk spilling
The patter of the cereal falling

The banging of the mum tripping
The squeaking of the door opening
The slamming of the door shutting
The brrr of the engine starting.

Vinal Patel (7)
Quinton House School, Upton

Household Soundtrack

The bubbling of the saucepan
The crackling of the fire
The squealing of the mice
The pinging of the wire

The rattling of the kettle
The singing of the thrush
The smashing of the glass
The swishing of the brush

The laughter of the children
The ticking of the clock
The ringing of the bell
The sizzling of the wok.

Oliver Strickland (7)
Quinton House School, Upton

Safari Sounds

The stamping of the elephant
The roaring of the lion
The cheekiness of the monkeys
The crunching of the bear

The squeaking of the birds
The tu-whit tu-whoo of the owls
The tiptoeing of the mouse
The pattering of the rain

The running of the children
The slithering of the snake
The howling of the wind
The banging of the doors.

Benjamin Willingham (7)
Quinton House School, Upton

JJ Horton

He's completely football crazy
And totally football mad
And his name is JJ Horton
But he's really not that bad.

He's going out with a girl called Michele
They have got two children too
One of them is Ellie Grace
And the other is Jessica Lou.

Now JJ plays for Blisworth
An ordinary football club
But the only problem is
Blisworth's got a pub.

Now JJ is getting older
And really rather tough
And sometimes when he is playing
He gets a bit too rough.

Ellie Horton (9)
Quinton House School, Upton

Lazy Daisy

There once was a cat called Daisy,
She plays with her best friend Maisy,
They play all day,
Apart from in May,
Cos that was the month they were lazy.

Sally Newton (10)
Quinton House School, Upton

Child And Dad

'I'm going to go and get something to eat.'
  'Why?'
'Because my stomach is growling.'
  'Why?'
'Because it needs food.'
  'Why?'
'Because I don't have any food in me.'
  'Why?'
'Because you won't let me go and get any food.'
  'Why?'
'I don't know.'
  'Why?'
'Just let me go and get some food.'
  'Why?'
'Because I will shrivel up and die.'
  'OK, bye-bye then.'

Oliver Bates (10)
Quinton House School, Upton

Why?

'I am going to the supermarket.'
'Why?'
'To get some stuff.'
'Why?'
'Because we are running out of food.'
'Why?'
'Isn't it high time you stopped saying why.'
'Why shall I stop saying why?'
'Because you're beginning to annoy me
with the word why anyway I am going bye.'

Jia Chadha (9)
Quinton House School, Upton

The School Bully

'Hello, Mrs Bullyfull, it's about your girl.'
'Which girl?'
'Your girl.'
'But which?'
'Oh her name, Rachel.'
'What's she done?'
'Well . . .
She beat up Jane,
Knocked out Sophie,
Chopped down a tree,
Poked the pet gerbil's eye,
Put a brick down the toilet.'
'But you're meant to!'
'Not in the bowl though!'
'Oh!'
'Also . . .
Skipped school for a month,
Left the tap running,
Threw a table at me.'
'Did she?'
Must be strong!'
'Very.'
'Well done to her.'
'She also . . .
Climbed over the gate,
Swore at Tom,
Shouted at Mrs Bluebell!'
'Who's she?'
'Teacher!'
'Oh no!'
'Oh yes!'
'Did she forgive herV'
'Yes, Mrs Bullyfull, but the children are scared of her!'
'Why?'
'She is a teacher!'

Sophie Blurton (9)
St Joseph's RC Junior School, Nuneaton

A Poemful Of Nouns

A rabble of rabbits racing around,
A skyful of snowflakes not making a sound,
A caravan of camels out for a caper,
An authority of authors writing on paper,
A package of princes preparing for a party,
A puddle of painters doing something arty,
A canter of kangaroos following larks,
A deluge of dolphins dodging sharks,
A ring of racoons outrunning ramblers,
A barrage of boys playing rock scramblers!

Emily Roberts (10)
St Peter's CE Primary School, Market Bosworth

Upside Down

When I'm hanging upside down
And not the right way round,
I look up at the clouds in the sky
And watch an aeroplane go by.

When I'm hanging upside down
And not the right way round,
I look up at the sky and use my imagination
To merge a cloud into a new creation.

When I'm hanging upside down
And not the right way round,
The different clouds remind me of things
Maybe one of them could be a bird with wings.

When I'm hanging upside down
And not the right way round,
I'm lying on my slide
About to glide down to the bottom again.

Hannah Williamson (11)
St Peter's CE Primary School, Market Bosworth

A Creepy House

A creepy house stands alone,
with a path covered in grass and stone.
A scary broomstick lies outside,
while a black cat stands next to its side.
Spooky pumpkins float in the sky,
they make other people pass by.
Broken stand there for all to see,
no one daren't go near that house, not even a bee.

Scott Cumbley (10)
St Peter's CE Primary School, Market Bosworth

My Dogs

My dogs sit upon my lap,
they also lie on their mats.
They really don't like cats,
they always chew my dad's hats.

My dogs always chase the sheep
but they never stray far from the Jeep.
They always listen to the whistle
but they're always careful of the thistle.

My dogs run through the grass
but they're always aware of glass.
They're always clever
as soft as a feather.

And I'll always love my dogs.

Hannah Ingham (9)
St Peter's CE Primary School, Market Bosworth

The Eve Of Hallowe'en

There's haunting faces at your door,
Ghosts, witches, Dracula and more.
'We've come to get you,' Dracula said.
'Oh sorry, can't come, it's time for my bed.'
When midnight came there was a full moon,
The wolves were out, they'll gobble you up soon.
I was lying in my bed at 2 o'clock,
When at the door there was a knock.
I got out of bed and answered it,
Oh my goodness, it was the wicked witch.

Renee Allen (10)
St Peter's CE Primary School, Market Bosworth

Stormy Night

I was in my bed on a stormy night
When the moon was shining bright
In the middle of the night.

I got out of bed
And banged my head on my bunk
And tripped over my trunk
And landed on my junk.

The junk was scattered everywhere
But I didn't care
I still went to the funfair in the middle of the night
When the moon was shining bright.

Samuel Ingham (9)
St Peter's CE Primary School, Market Bosworth

My Elephant

My elephant is big,
He acts like a pig,
He loves to play ping-pong,
Whilst singing a song.

He likes sporty things,
To do wearing wings,
He is very scary and strong,
He likes trying fluffy pink clothes on.

He loves going out to dinner,
He's always called the best winner,
He's got lots of friends,
He's very crazy, round the bend.

Niamh Gascoyne (9)
St Peter's CE Primary School, Market Bosworth

Sleepover

My friends came over one dark night,
The bestest bit was the pillow fight,
I scared them all with wicked dares,
I'm not surprised they had nightmares.

In the morning when we woke,
We got out of bed and something broke,
I felt under my bed
And out poked a doll's head.

When it was time to say goodbye,
There was no need for sorrows, so we didn't cry,
We've had lots of fun and things you like,
Like playing scrabble and riding your bike.

Mary Pegg (8)
St Peter's CE Primary School, Market Bosworth

The Devil

In the Underworld the Devil causes misery,
His pet is a bear, very grizzly.
He tortures everyone with a whip,
You better not give him any lip.
He will scare the living daylights out of you,
Sadly it's true.
He can count in treble,
After all he is the Devil.

Ben Swan (10)
St Peter's CE Primary School, Market Bosworth

My Dog

My dog is cool,
My dog is a fool,
I love my dog,
In a different way,
My dog is insane,
My dog is a pain.

My dog likes playing in the sun,
My dog likes to have a bun,
My dog likes playing with a stone,
My dog likes knocking gnomes,
My dog likes playing outside,
My dog likes pushing me down the slide.

Sophie Lacey (9)
St Peter's CE Primary School, Market Bosworth

My Dogs

Kim

Ankle biter
Foot licker
Sheep rounder
Rabbit chaser
Biscuit gobbler
Football popper

Missy

Tile wee-er
Squeaky barker
Carpet scratcher
Slow eater
Ball chomper.

Emma Francis-Scott (10)
St Peter's CE Primary School, Market Bosworth

My Rabbit

M y rabbit's name is Hutch,
Y esterday he ate six carrots.

R an around the garden 16 times,
A nd then he got really dizzy,
B ut then he came inside,
B ut then he did something disgusting on me,
I t was horrible,
T hen I had a bath.

Abigail Cresswell (9)
St Peter's CE Primary School, Market Bosworth

Winter Morning

Cold mornings, dark and crisp
Blankets warm as toast
Keeping me in bed
Comfortable
'Time to get up!' comes the call
Further under the covers I go
Snuggling down
I don't want to go to school
'Time to get up!'
It comes again
The shrill voice has no effect
The marshmallow mattress sucks me in
The cotton wool pillow hugs me
Like a warm cloud around my ears
'Get up it's snowing!' the voice hollers
'The radio said no school today!'
Out of bed in flash
Down the stairs
Pulling on clothes
Outside in a nano-second
Who wants to waste the day in bed?
It's snowballing time!

Lucy Sandford-James (10)
St Peter's CE Primary School, Market Bosworth

Snowflakes

Snowflakes swirling,
Round and round,
Landing softly on the ground,
Snowflakes make crispy snow,
That children played in long ago.

Jessica Hurst (7)
St Peter's CE Primary School, Market Bosworth

Flowers

Flowers, flowers standing in a row
Flowers, flowers help them to grow
Flowers, flowers as beautiful as you can see
Flowers, flowers I love them and they love me.

Romey Kinsella (7)
St Peter's CE Primary School, Market Bosworth

Family Happiness

Happiness is cuddling up to Mum
On a chilly winter's night
By the fireside and watching
A weepy film

Happiness is striding out with Dad
Across fields in wellington boots
On a cold morning and looking
For animal tracks

Happiness is playing with your sister
In the garden on a summer's day
Bouncing on the trampoline
And chasing her

Happiness is listening to Grandma
Telling stories of the olden days
Hearing about Grandad's life
When he was young

Happiness is having your family around
And knowing that they love you
Always, forever, no matter what
You ever do.

Anna Sandford-James (10)
St Peter's CE Primary School, Market Bosworth

The Martian

It was just last week,
When I woke up one morn
And walked down the stairs
And I could've sworn

That there on the sofa,
With six great green warts,
Was an alien, no a Martian,
Not tall, but quite short.

It then got quite frightened,
And I suddenly knew why,
The slippers Gran gave me
For my birthday in July!

The scream that it made,
Sending chills down my spine,
The look on my face
But it really didn't mind.

Then suddenly, pop!
It exploded to dust,
My mum called from the kitchen,
'Don't make such a fuss!'

So that was my tale
Of a Martian that morning,
My friends in my class said,
'Well that is just boring.'

Helena Parkes (10)
St Peter's CE Primary School, Market Bosworth

Football

Arsenal are the best by far
Owen is Newcastle's star
Footballers have beautiful houses
Barcelona own a lot of trousers

Rooney has a lot of love
Crouch's head is so above
Ronaldo has a giant wig
Dida likes playing tig

Steve McClaren has the groove
Sven Goran Eriksson can't move
David James is such a thug
Ashley Cole's phone has a bug.

Owen Hills (10)
St Peter's CE Primary School, Market Bosworth

The Sky!

The sky in the day is clear and blue,
Beautiful food you'll munch and chew,
A colourful rainbow fills the air,
Fantastic looks you'll soon be there.

Lambs fill the grassy meadows on the land,
Down on the beach I see a pile of sand,
The sky at night is dark and gloomy,
But the inspiring heavens are vast and roomy.

Lilies grow on a lake,
On some grass lays a rake,
Velvety clouds up very high,
So I feel I can almost touch the sky!

Harriet Ball (9)
St Peter's CE Primary School, Market Bosworth

England Poem

England are good
and England should
win Euro 2008
but they mustn't be late

Joe Cole scored a great goal
then he was sent to the North Pole
and fell in a giant rabbit hole
Then he drowned
and England won the second round.

Harry Saunders (9)
St Peter's CE Primary School, Market Bosworth

The Icy Mountain

The snowy grass had laid itself around the mountainous mountain.
It was cold, crispy grass and it was wrapping itself around
the thick, stiff, tanned bronze-coloured mud.
The immense, lifeless trees killed by the coldness were scattered
all over the emerald-coloured grass.
They were dark beige trees that towered over you.
The mountain was gargantuan and rocky and it soared over you
when you went near it.
The layers of freezing snow coated the mountain like it was a magnet
to a piece of metal.

Luke Batham (9)
St Peter's CE Primary School, Market Bosworth

Goal!

Now Chelsea have a problem with A Cole
Cause he's built a home in the North Pole
He's not allowed to play
Unless Chelsea give him a holiday.

Now Cech and Cudicini are both out injured
Roman Abramovich has been ningered
Abramovich has loads of money
But his mum thinks it's really funny

Now Arsenal have a problem with their form
And people say they sleep in a dorm
But that's not true
And Tottenham players have the flu.

France, well the name says it, 'France'
They all dance in pink fluffy pants
Well apart from Henry
Who is the French fondie!

Curtis Taylor (9)
St Peter's CE Primary School, Market Bosworth

The Save

There I was in the final of the World Cup
The score was 3-3 for the cup
It went to penalties
Thierry Henry takes a shot
I dived up and up then I saved it
We had won the World Cup
The joy that filled my heart
The crowd came running on the pitch
We had won.

Peter Harle (10)
St Peter's CE Primary School, Market Bosworth

What Is Pink?

Pink is the colour of smelly pig
Pink is the colour of curly wigs
Pink is the colour of ballerinas
Pink is the colour of disco divas
Pink is the colour of pink lipstick
Pink is the colour of a lolly you lick.

Darcie Finn (7)
St Peter's CE Primary School, Market Bosworth

The Football Match

The crowd is yawning,
'It's time for a goal.'
So Joe Cole,
Goes up to the goal,
He shoots, he scores.
The crowd is praying,
While the football band
Starts playing!
'It's A Miracle'.

Chloe McDougall (10)
St Peter's CE Primary School, Market Bosworth

The Mammoth Mansion

On a moonlit hill at the end of the Earth stood a dark
And shadowy mansion.
In the bowels of the basement lurked a creature
Named Hark Bansion.
On special occasions he roamed round above
And on special occasions he attacked doves.
Other animals lurked in the dark,
Some of them looked just like a shark.
Some were tall, some were small,
Some were shaped just like a ball.
Some were hairy, some were scary,
One was named Jonathan Vary.
But when the sun shone really bright,
The creatures could not stand the light.
This is a brief description of the mansion
And the creatures within, one of them named Hark Bansion.

Joseph Bibby (9)
St Peter's CE Primary School, Market Bosworth

Sky

When the day turns into night,
I switch on the pumpkin lights,
When the sky turned dark and black,
I may just turn my back.

When it's day but the sky is black,
No one is going to come back,
When it's clear I am fine,
My brother is on the line.

When it's blue I am good,
You won't like it but I would,
When it's cloudy, it is grey,
How am I going to pay?

Sam Marston (9)
St Peter's CE Primary School, Market Bosworth

The Moshing Crowd

The band exploded with amazing tunes while the crowd moshed
like crazy lunes.

I cheered as the band played and played,
The crowd roared like a mad parade.
I jumped as the band rocked and rolled,
I saw in front of me, a man that was bald.
After the band finished their play,
The neighbours shouted, 'Hooray!'

Ali Clinton (10)
St Peter's CE Primary School, Market Bosworth

Who Am I?

Letter taker,
Child waker,
Kitchen cook,
Take a look,
Who is it?
My mum.

Factory worker,
Road runner,
Late sleeper,
Great keeper,
Who is it?
My dad.

Sister teaser,
Teacher pleaser,
Goal smasher,
Ball smacker,
Who is it?
My brother.

Noise maker,
Finger sucker,
Tower builder,
Cot sleeper,
Who is it?
My little sister.

This is my family.

Kelly Pyne (10)
Shipston-On-Stour J&I School, Shipston-On-Stour

The Unusual Baboon

Once there was a baboon called Charlie,
Who was a big fan of Bob Marley.
He played all his tapes
And laughed at the apes
And rode astride on his Harley . . .

. . . Davidson I mean!

James Hudson (10)
Shipston-On-Stour J&I School, Shipston-On-Stour

Limerick

There once was a tiger called Bob
Who had a very interesting job,
He lived in a zoo
With a fish called Sue
And she was a bit of a snob.

Ellie Turner (10)
Shipston-On-Stour J&I School, Shipston-On-Stour

Anger

Anger is metal melting and boiling.
Anger feels like burning hot coal being pressed against bare skin.
It tastes like bitter lemon gnawing at your screaming tonsils.
It looks like a rocky volcano smothered in scalding hot lava.
Anger is like blazing flames rising and spitting in a pitch-black night.
It is the colour of blood oozing out of an open wound.
It smells like smoke swimming out of the light of a smouldering bonfire.

Olivia West (10)
Shipston-On-Stour J&I School, Shipston-On-Stour

Emotions

Fear is the sound of a train hooting as it enters a tunnel,
Fear is the smell of a burning gas,
Fear is the taste of a sour lemon,
Fear is the touch of a spiky cactus,
Fear is the colour of a rough sea flag,
Fear is cowering!

Anger is the sound of an elephant,
Anger is the smell of a hot chilli,
Anger is the taste of a sour unripe plum,
Anger is the touch of a smouldering metal,
Anger is the colour of a stream of crimson red blood,
Anger is hottening!

Silence is the sound of sorrow,
Silence is the smell of fresh air,
Silence is the taste of fresh mints,
Silence is the touch of a book,
Silence is the colour of a blank page,
Silence is calming!

Jealousy is the sound of a gremlin,
Jealousy is the smell of hot metal,
Jealousy is the taste of an orange,
Jealousy is the touch of a clump of dust,
Jealousy is the colour of a blank night sky,
Jealousy is weakening!

Happiness is the sound of a tweeting bird at dawn,
Happiness is the smell of freshly baked bread,
Happiness is the taste of heavenly milk chocolate,
Happiness is the touch of a silky dress,
Happiness is the colour of the sunset,
Happiness is warming!

Emily Jennings (11)
Shipston-On-Stour J&I School, Shipston-On-Stour

I Am Mother Earth

I have given you family and friends to love,
I have given you mountains and rivers,
I have given you food and water,
I have given you air to breathe,
I have given you nature to admire.

I am tolerant when people break up,
I am tolerant when pollution is surrounding me,
I am tolerant when people don't recycle,
I am tolerant when you let bombs hit me.

I show I'm angry when I shoot out my lava from volcanoes,
I show I'm angry when I shake my body,
I show I'm angry when I strike lightning,
I am Mother Earth, respect me please.

Erinn Melville (8)
Stanley Road Primary School, Worcester

I Am Mother Earth

I have given you houses to live in,
I have given you families to love,
I have given you food to eat.

I am tolerant when people fight,
I am tolerant when people throw rubbish in the sea,
I am tolerant when people throw bombs.

I show anger when horrible earthquakes knock houses down,
I show anger when there is no rain and water for people to drink,
I show anger when houses blow away.

I am Mother Earth, please take care of me.

Sadikur Rahman (8)
Stanley Road Primary School, Worcester

I Am Mother Earth

I have given you rain so your plants can grow,
I have given you houses so you can have shelter,
I have given you trees for shade.

I am tolerant when bombs kill people,
I am tolerant when people throw litter,
I am tolerant when there are no trees.

I show anger when there are volcanoes shooting lava in the air,
I show anger when there is no water,
I show anger when there are earthquakes breaking the ground.

I am Mother Earth, please don't hurt me.

Alizah Parveen Ghalib (7)
Stanley Road Primary School, Worcester

I Am The Earth

I am the Earth
I am kind because I give you lovely fresh air
I give you plants and trees that give you food
I am kind because I give you soil to grow your food

I am the Earth
I am tolerant because I put up with you throwing rubbish on the floor
And in the rivers, seas and canals
I put up with you calling names and shooting each other
I put up with bombs that damage me
I put up with people killing animals for skin rugs
And their heads to hang up for decorations
For killing elephants for their tusks and rhinos for their horns
I don't treat you like this
I have had enough

I am the Earth
I am angry because you treat me like a piece of dirt
I give you tsunamis that wash away houses, towns and cities
I kill people with this
I give you earthquakes turning buildings to rubble
I give you hurricanes and tornadoes spinning around
At amazing speeds
I give you storms with thunder and lightning
And floods that wash you and your crops away.

So, I want you to treat me carefully and with respect
Because I am your Earth
I am the Earth.

Sam Savage (8) & Joseph Sartain (7)
Stanley Road Primary School, Worcester

I Am The Earth

I am the Earth
I am the kind Earth
I give you water
I give you food
I also provide jungles, mountains and fields.

I am the Earth
I am tolerant, I am tolerant of the abusive way I am treated
By the people I created
People drop rubbish
Drop bombs
Kill animals
Pollute the water, the land
Pollute the air we breathe.

I am the Earth
I am angry
I punish people
I send tornadoes and hurricanes
Great floods and earthquakes.

So, maybe you people will listen and be good
And treat things perfectly.

Ryan Brookes (8)
Stanley Road Primary School, Worcester

I Am Mother Earth

I have given you oxygen and air,
I have given you a family to love you,
I have given you a friend to play with.

I am tolerant when your smoke goes in the air,
I am tolerant when the pipes go through me,
I am tolerant when your environment kills animals.

I show anger when lightning flashes and thunder roars,
I show anger when my volcano bursts with lava,
I show anger when the sea is like a monster.

I am Mother Earth, please look after me.

Jacob Moseley (8)
Stanley Road Primary School, Worcester

Witches' Lullaby

Witches' broths aren't all that rare,
they contain a big handful of matted horsehair.
You also need crispy rust from old tools,
not forgetting the two pairs of juicy rats' eyeballs.
Toenail clippings, they need to be crushed,
105 grams of dandruff, add water until mushed.
You have to find six monkey tails,
usually found in vampire sales.
Then stir it in with really no care,
for good luck, give it one almighty evil stare.
Let it splish and let it splosh,
then pinch your neighbour's giant moustache.
Finally add sticky earwax, 636 grams at the max.
You need to beware,
so don't declare anything rare,
like the fact that you could be a witch!
Humans are about, so have no doubt that,
they could find your broth, any time, any time soon
and have it for tea by mistake!
Urgh, yuck.

Charlotte May (10)
The Ferncumbe CE Primary School, Hatton

My Pet Cat Slick

My pet cat Slick,
Black and quick,
Smooth and furry,
She's so purry,
She's so soft
And always in the loft,
Clawing the bed by my Ted.

Tazmin Pinfold (9)
The Ferncumbe CE Primary School, Hatton

Hush, Hush

What was that Grandma?
It's only a storm, hush, hush.
The storm roared just like a lion,
What was that Grandma?
It's only a storm, hush, hush.
Bang! Bang!
It was like an elephant on the roof,
What was that Grandma?
It's only a storm, hush, hush.
Whack, whack on the window,
It was the whipping trees,
What was that Grandma?
It's only a storm, hush, hush.
There was a massive uproar,
The tree had fallen,
They were both dead.
Hush, hush, it was only a storm!

Ben Johnson (10)
The Ferncumbe CE Primary School, Hatton

My Hamster

My hamster is so sweet,
I am so lucky, he is a treat.

My hamster sometimes bites
And doesn't come out if there's lights.

My hamster is sometimes smelly,
He eats a lot so has a very big belly!

He is always eating and never stops,
So he really loves his chocolate drops.

He sleeps a lot, all day in fact (if I don't wake him up),
But he really has a big impact.

He is grey and brown and has a big pink nose
And he is always doing the teddy bear pose.
Awww!

Naomi Cruden (11)
The Ferncumbe CE Primary School, Hatton

Hush, It's Only The Storm

"What's that roaring like a lion?'
'Hush, it's only the storm.'

What's that twirling round and round?'
'Hush, it's only the storm.'

'What's that coming over the hill?'
'Hush, it's only the storm.'

'What's that breaking all the roofs?'
'Hush, it's only the storm.'

'It's like a herd of raging bulls.'
'Hush, it's only the storm.'

'That was like something I'd never seen before.'
'Hush, it's only the storm.'

Connor Henman (10)
The Ferncumbe CE Primary School, Hatton

Monster Lullaby

Come, get to bed,
do this instead
of playing outside,
when the humans are out
they'll think you're scary,
then it will be wary
and ruined forever,
so save it for Hallowe'en
when the monster king
rules the land.
Then humans will think
we're dressed up,
covered in powdery make-up,
don't go outside,
we have to stay in and hide!

Amelia Morris (9)
The Ferncumbe CE Primary School, Hatton

The Ship In The Dark

In the haunted ship
That's terrorised by ghosts
And monsters of the dark

The swimming pool steaming
With the wet empty path
And dead bodies screaming
In the dark

A fireball screeching towards you
Its flames engulfing your body
A deep, scary, horrifying face
Grinning, at the moment it kills you

The hull is being torn
And dead bodies are born
The dead ones
Begging you not to leave
In the dark

Ghosts screaming at you
Tearing your soul
And killing you in the darkness
Of the ghost ship, in the dark.

Daniel Ingall-Tombs (10)
The Ferncumbe CE Primary School, Hatton

10 Things Found In A Wizard's Pocket

A huge lion made of silk.
A magic spell book on a multicoloured shelf.
A jar of bad foolish thoughts and spells.
A bad-tempered fairy covered in a black cloak.
An apple that can talk in a very low and loud voice.
A purple, red and black dragon that has only got one wing and eye.
Pinocchio with a nose as tall as a tower.
A poisonous potion that is red and green to stop Christmas
from coming.
Stars that spring up by the moon.
An enchanted tree that stands in the land of sweets and cake.

Harriet Goucher (8)
Winterfold House School, Chaddesley

The Storm

The owls were hooting as I went to bed
I snuggled up tight with little Ted
I could hear the dog whining in amazement

I could hear thunder growling
Its way through the night
Flash, crash, a lightning strike
Our dear cat had a terrible night

The waves were crashing
The windows were bashing
As the fishing boats rocked to the beat.

Phoebe Lydon (10)
Winterfold House School, Chaddesley

Ted

(Who jumped on his bed and suffered a chaotic catastrophe of great enormity)

There was a boy called Ted
Who loved to jump on his bed,
He'd bounce all day and night
Giving his mother a fright.
But, when in warning she shouted
Ted just moaned and pouted,
Not taking heed of the warning
When he should have been in bed yawning,
He was jumping up and down,
He was the happiest boy in town.
With joy he jumped even higher,
It was all the fun he could desire.
But as the night grew late
To the boy I do relate,
A great misfortune befell
And to those who in that house did dwell.
Ted's head went through the ceiling,
So he began feeling
Quite awful as he called
To his parents who were appalled,
But still came to Ted's lair
And then, I am dreadfully afraid,
Due to all the pulling and tugging
And after his parents shrugging,
The ceiling came down and fell,
Despite many a yell,
Upon the floor below
Breaking every window.
Then the bed went through the floor,
Neighbours came out of their front door
To see what was going on.
With the weight of over a ton
The family lay under the house.

Nothing survived, not even a mouse,
Ted and his family were now all dead
Because of him jumping on a bed!

Moral:

The moral is that children like Ted
Should never ever jump on their bed.

Lydia Brindley (11)
Winterfold House School, Chaddesley

Ebenezer Scrooge

Ebenezer Scrooge was a cold-hearted fool
He never spent money, misery was his tool
His eyes held the warmth of a dead man's gaze
His lips were as pinched as the winter days
His nose was as hooked as a vulture's claw
The skin was cracked, red and raw
Everyone hid when Scrooge came past
Wishing this winter would be his last!

Sophie Grenfell (10)
Winterfold House School, Chaddesley

Grace

(The girl who loved to pull a horrible face)

There once was a little girl called Grace
Who loved to pull a horrid face
It was in fact a Thursday
When her auntie came to stay
Grace twisted her face into yet another gruesome shape
Her mother kept quiet, so she would not wake
But failed
When her auntie saw her niece she wailed
Then fainted clean away
And went home that very day
Young Grace went outside, still wearing the face
That would disgrace the entire human race
It just so happened that there was wind
And this little girl's face began to change
Her eyes and nose were rearranged
She looked in the mirror in the bathroom
And knew her mother would find out soon
Her face was twisted round and round
Her nose and mouth looked like they were bound
The glass began to crack
And fell on the floor with a smack
Now poor Grace wears a paper bag
Upon her head, and her dog's tail does not wag.

The moral:
The moral of this story is that you should not pull silly faces
Or you will end up like poor Grace is.

Mary Shinner (10)
Winterfold House School, Chaddesley

Ted

(He refused to go to bed and ended up dead!)

It was always young Ted
Who never went to bed,
So when he went to school
He looked like a fool
Because of his skinny pale head.

He had dark bags under his eyes
And could even have won a prize
For the funniest face
Ever seen in this dull place,
That would always make children slap thighs.

He now wanted revenge
On those who he thought were his friends,
So he conjured a plan
That was scary for even a man
And would make all the laughing end.

Ted didn't listen to his mother's warning,
When suddenly he started yawning,
He went in a daydream into the street
Where was knocked off his feet
And nobody heard him calling.

He would've dressed like a ghoul
And made them all look like fools,
If it weren't for the bus
That hit him and thus,
Created a huge blood pool.

Sam Price (10)
Winterfold House School, Chaddesley

Jamaica

Below the USA is the island of Jamaica,
Among its mountains are huge palm tree forests,
In the forests are scarlet red parrots and rushing falls,
On the flat grounds are white beaches and great hotels,
By them are the calm, turquoise waters of the Caribbean,
Beneath the water colourful fish dart about.
Above all this, a paraglider soars through the sky,
Over him, a fiery gleaming sun looks down on the island.

Sam Young (9)
Winterfold House School, Chaddesley

A Viking Limerick

There was a young Viking from York
Whose leg was stabbed with a fork
They chopped it off at the knee
Then gave him some tea
And now he always stands like a stork.

Adam Grenfell (9)
Winterfold House School, Chaddesley

A Viking Limerick

There was a young Viking from Norway
Who decided to leave home and run away
He went to the pub
To get some grub
And now he is too full to run away.

Jordan White (10)
Winterfold House School, Chaddesley

A Viking Limerick

There was a young Viking from York
Who was particularly keen on roast pork
He ate with a spoon
But he finished too soon
So now he always uses a table fork.

Katie Jeffries (9)
Winterfold House School, Chaddesley

Spring

Nights will get lighter
Flowers and plants brighter
Everything starts growing
Grass will soon need mowing

Birds start to sing
When it turns to spring
Children start to play
Soon it will be the month of May

The sun will shine brighter
The nights will be lighter
Kites will start to fly
In the beautiful blue sky.

Elliott Hunt (9)
Winterfold House School, Chaddesley

The Storm

We went out in a boat on the sea
My mum and dad and me
We all left at about three
The sea was calm and quiet
As we left the harbour riot

Then suddenly there was a rumble
The big dials took a tumble
Form side to side and up and down
Around and around like a merry-go-round

The wind began to howl
Daddy gave a big scowl
We had better head home
Before we reach Rome

The harbour was very near
We all gave a great cheer
We had beaten the storm
Soon we were home in the warm.

Jess Morris (11)
Winterfold House School, Chaddesley

The Storm

The sky grew dark
And dogs began to bark
And the wind whistled through the trees

Down poured the rain
The thunder crashed
And bright lightning flashed

A branch fell from a tree
Narrowly missing me
As I ran along the track
There was another thunder crack

I ran all the way home
In puddles I splashed
As the lightning flashed

I reached my door
Just as the rain began to pour
Soon the storm would end
And the damage we would mend.

George Goucher (9)
Winterfold House School, Chaddesley

The Storm

I was lying in my bed watching the lightning
My dogs thought it all very frightening
Outside it was dark
It made Ollie and Max bark

Clattering doors and dirty paws
Mum shouting come indoors
Roaring thunder in the sky
Big black clouds floating up high.

Joseph Taylor (10)
Winterfold House School, Chaddesley

The Storm

One stormy night it was frosty and cold
Two small children had to be brave and bold
Thunder boomed in the midnight sky
It scared the children who thought they would die

The storm grew louder and louder with each passing hour
Then the rain came down in a sudden shower
Lightning flashed at hyper speed
It happened so fast I gave a loud scream

Mum hugged us so tight
We suddenly needed it that night
For deep down inside we feared that night
We'd all had a terrible fright.

Benjamin Melamed (10)
Winterfold House School, Chaddesley

A Viking Limerick

There was a young Viking from Norway
Who sailed his ship one May day
Passing land far and wide
On the tip of the tide
He shouted hip hip, hip hip hooray.

Christian Weston (9)
Winterfold House School, Chaddesley

A Viking Limerick

There was a young Viking from Peru
Who liked to eat pizza and sticky goo
But when they ran out
He gave a big shout
And said, 'Now what else can I chew?'

Elliott Price (9)
Winterfold House School, Chaddesley

A Viking Limerick

There was a young Viking from York
Who really liked his roast pork
He ate a whole pig
And grew very big
And got stuck in the door like a cork.

Axel Taylor (9)
Winterfold House School, Chaddesley

A Viking Limerick

There was a young Viking from France
Who wanted to learn how to dance
He trod on a cat
And turned into a bat
And now walks around in black pants.

Matthew Bubb (9)
Winterfold House School, Chaddesley

A Viking Limerick

There was a young Viking from Rhyll
Who would always get a big thrill
By going around
With a big hound
And would refuse to settle his bill.

Alesha Kettle (10)
Winterfold House School, Chaddesley

A Viking Limerick

There was a young Viking from Crewe
Who loved a pretty girl called Sue
They went on a ship
For a short trip
Visiting an island with a real igloo.

Harry Hawkeswood (10)
Winterfold House School, Chaddesley

A Viking Limerick

There was a young Viking from Spain
Who never used to like the rain
He shouted out loud
'I can see a cloud'
Before he went to hide in a drain.

Jack Barwell (9)
Winterfold House School, Chaddesley

A Viking Limerick

There was a young Viking from the town
Who hopped, jumped and fell down
He broke all his toes
And his big nose
But did not hurt his hard crown.

Cameron Bales (9)
Winterfold House School, Chaddesley

A Viking Limerick

There was a young Viking from Norway
Who fell right through the doorway
He broke all his toes
And even his nose
That silly young Viking from Norway.

Joseph Stringer (9)
Winterfold House School, Chaddesley

A Viking Limerick

There was a young Viking from Norway
Who liked to jig in the doorway
He said, 'I'm going to dance
All the way to France
But, I'd rather just have a play day.'

Luke Staniland (10)
Winterfold House School, Chaddesley

Young Writers Information

We hope you have enjoyed reading this book - and that you will continue to enjoy it in the coming years.

If you like reading and writing poetry drop us a line, or give us a call, and we'll send you a free information pack.

Alternatively if you would like to order further copies of this book or any of our other titles, then please give us a call or log onto our website at www.youngwriters.co.uk

Young Writers Information
Remus House
Coltsfoot Drive
Peterborough
PE2 9JX

(01733) 890066